Tales of

Giselle Reyna

| a collection of poetry and prose |

stars filled the sky
as I start to cry
and you dried them with just your smile

- *ones smile*

i let myself fall for you
because i knew..
like i told you before
it's always going to be you.
years later we're here in this room
saying our vows
and all the I do's

- *since forever*

love me harder
and hold on tighter
when we are struggling to keep it together

- *the tides*

going through changes
and phases
and trying to keep a relationship
is tough,
but it seems so easy with you

- *minutes passing*

you don't have to hold back tears
or hold back your hurt
the love that we share is stronger than our downfalls

- *free*

minutes passed
days passed
months passed
and years passed
but you remained in love with me

- *clock*

Every love song reminds me of you

-   *radio*

just like the tree next to an old farm
lonely,
just like I,
hoping to be found by someone or something
and one day, many people began to surround this tree
as if it were special
just the way I feel when I'm with you
"someone wants me"
that's what goes through my head…
happiness.
love

- *not alone anymore*

I know I love you because I would do anything just to see a smile on your face
I know I love you because I'll sacrifice myself for you to be safe
I know I love you because I reminisce a future with you
I know I love you because when your hurting it hurts me too
I know I love you because this is about you

- *best for you*

I remember when I did that
I put my hand on your cheek telling you it's going to
be okay
I loved you in your pain no matter how hard it was
on you
I remember when my hand went down your arm to
hold your hand
my hands always cold and yours always there to
keep me warm
you would look at me like you were lucky so lucky
that you would try your best to stay
cause I was always yours
I wrote this hoping you never want to let me go

-   *endless*

And i wonder if there's a time
when I wake up and see you in
our my bed with lazy eyes
I want you here

- *you is what I need*

I just hope that one day
you say you wanna change my last name.

-   *high hopes*

my heart still longs for his love
my body still craves for his touch
my hands still write the feeling of how he made me
feel
he shows up in my dreams from time to time and my
soul never wants to awake
every key on the piano reminds me of how he used to
play for me
every smile he gives me has me smiling all day
every tear that has fell from my eyes he has washed
away
even though we were struggling to keep ourselves
together in the relationship we still fought for each
other because we loved each other
and although we're apart now without choice
we still cheer on one another
loving each other from a far is what we've been
doing until it's our time to meet again I'll continue to
cheer him on from here

-   *here we are*

you don't have to wait for me
   I'm all yours

-    *7/16*

I've spent countless hours thinking about what
would've happened if I didn't have you

   -   *glad your here*

here missing you more than ever

- *beach vibes*

waiting patiently for the day you…

- *days, weeks, months, years*

only a few days more then I could have you in my
arms
hold your hand
and love you more

- *8/12*

I'm longing for the day you say
"honey I'm home"

- *Long days*

late night talks
watching movies all night
laughing together
and me admiring you for being mine

- *Together*

"Mom" being the first word he's said
him giving another women his love
his mother happy for him but misses him
the women loving his mother for raising the best
guy she's ever met

-   *her story with him*

I love him more than this universe

-   *everybody knows*

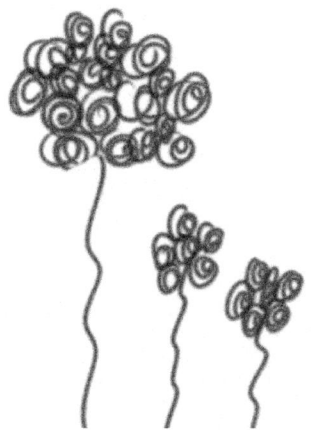

I love the way he holds me
I love the way he cares
I love the way he listens
I love all of him
because he loves all of me

- *the guy who loves my flaws*

they say they know your in love with me by the way
you look at me.

-   *Your eyes*

I never felt such a deep connection with someone
until I found you
and it makes me feel as if you are the only one who
understands me

-   *the castle on the mountain*

Feeling your touch
Escapes me from the world.
only you can make me feel that way

-   *gentleness*

I know I make you feel some type of way by the way you love me

- *everything you do*

spending a whole week with you was a week I will
never forget
you had me in the clouds

-   *with you*

The life i had before you is something I never want to go back to, so when you came into my life and brought the good out of me I knew I couldn't let that go, and I still have you and I can't image having anyone else

-   *changed me*

I wanted to stay in your arms forever

- *attached*

feeling the love and the emotions of having someone like you in my life is special

- *care for you*

you help me defeat the hardest moments of my life
and your always there for the grand moments
thank you…

-   *you stayed*

you make me so happy you don't understand..
my heart loves you more than anything in this world
I can't even describe how I feel next to you

-   *you're home*

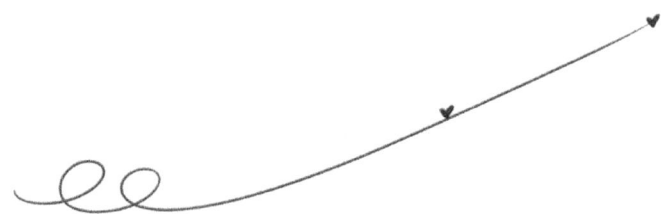

I always look forward to the days I get to see you

-   *you are*

I'm mesmerized by the way you love

-   *my fascination*

I never knew someone could love me so deeply till I
found you
words can't describe how it feels to be loved by you.

- *feel that way*

my hand fell between yours,
perfectly,
just like the night sky and stars.
holding your hand made me feel fortunate to even
have you

- *Us*

the memory of you looking at me is a memory I wish
you could see

-   *sketch book*

blessed to have someone that has cheered me up
when I was hurting.
I love you for that.

-    *appreciated*

I never seen a guy treat a girl like you do.

-   *your different*

The kind of guy I see in movies is the kind of guy I have loving me in the real world

- *no more fairytales*

you always loved me
even when it was hard to love myself
you cared for me
when I couldn't care for myself
You always waited for me
when I needed space
and I'll do the same for you as long as I live.

-   *that kind of love*

the heart beat I hear when my head is on your chest
reminds me of what I'm living for

- *Symphony*

you brought me out of my worst days and helped me
be the girl I always wanted to be
just thought you should know..

-   *secure*

how Noah loved Allie is how you love me..

- *compassionate*

I can't believe we're here together after waiting for
so long.
You were worth waiting for

-   *this one room*

you brought me peace whenever I needed it..

-   you're everything

when our eyes meet my heart goes wild
what we have is real wow..

- *I got my wish*

I wish I could explain to you how I feel

-   *sorry*

you could tell me you love me a million times but I
will never understand why

- *lo que siento*

my heart is full of misconceptions but when it's around you it can't help but know true love

-   *familiar place*

I want to be what you can't believe is yours

- *Wildest dream*

I never had anyone be as crazy for me as you

-   *getting used to*

there is something about how you look at me that
makes my voice tremble
and when you hug me I never want to let go
The way our hands a-line gives me chills down my
spine
I've never felt like this before, about anyone

-   *True loves touch*

I waited for many years for you
and I'll wait many more to be yours.

- *so close*

I don't think anyone could love you like I do.
I could make you smile from miles away
and make you feel like your in the clouds by just
looking into your eyes
I just hope I could make you feel like that forever…

-   *you feel*

my mind is like a river full of your love that flows constantly

-   *don't ever stop*

many people you've met,
and pretty faces you've seen,
and you still choose me

-   *the chosen*

I could admire you all day.

-   *sunset*

i want you to be the person I walk down the aisle with..

- *wd*

I want to do life with you
because you make me the happiest girl

- *big big plans*

Today was a day I will never for get
music, dancing
and you my by side

-   *10/8/21*

who am I if i don't have you.
A star who doesn't have a moon?
A mind without love?
A garden without flowers?
A forest without trees?
my love stay please..

- *mother nature*

many love poems I've wrote about you made me fall
more in love with you

- *truly yours*

I enjoy every moment with you even if you don't think I do

- *everything*

Have you ever been in love? Because I have, the first time I saw you, that day we met after waiting for so long had happiness written all over.

-    *Our love aligned*

a person without someone to love
Is like a turtle without its shell

-   *takes 2*

things about you make me wonder if any other girl
will be lucky enough to find

-   *one good prayer*

I wish there was more guys like you,
sweet, charming and respectful,
so every girl could get treated like royalty.

-   *sad*

could you hold my hand forever…

- *willingness*

Your the person I needed when I didn't know how to
deal with pain on my own

-   *can't thank you enough*

I find it crazy how someone like you
could love me

- *he sent you for me*

hold onto me
i need you

- *falling*

could you still love me even when I'm at my weakest
points?

- *the question*

the more I'm with you the less i feel lost in my
thoughts

-   *more truth*

i can't describe how I felt today with you
let's just say it was an unforgettable day
… it felt magical

- *with you*

i hope you never forget how I loved you.

- *continuously*

your past
isn't me
Im here to stay.

- *always will*

struggles are something we're going to go through.
I rather go through them with you than anyone else

- *easy on me*

you are what my heart needs

- *choose you*

i could come to you when I'm at my worst I know that.
I just never thought I'd have that at such a young age
but here we are…

-   *202005*

oh I love your kisses

-   *never too much*

i can't stop thinking about you..
you bring out the best of me
how could I not

-   *all the time*

our love for each other grows stronger every day

-   *love songs*

i don't want to rush this because I want us to last forever

- *eternity*

my love, you are the one for me
I want you
just you

-   *single peace*

i don't ever want to see you with anybody else

- *jealousy*

you should know how much I'm in love with you by everything I do.

-   *recognize*

I want to live in the moment wherever you stand

-   *no place like you*

I could stare into your eyes forever

-   *a life time*

you're more than just a guy
your the guy that could make a girl smile till her last
breath
your the only guy she's ever loved
and your the only guy she wants

-   *i choose you*

"I didn't want to let your hand go" you said,
I want us to be in love like this till there's nothing
left.

-   *sweaty palms*

your hand went along my skin slowly and gently
your touch is what I crave

- *chills*

my heart goes crazy when you kiss me

-   *sweet like honey*

don't be sorry for giving me the best thing in the world
…
your love

- red

you are breathtaking

- *Collapse*

the first time I laid on your shoulder
was the time I felt safety
haven't felt that in a while

- *small black couch*

there is nothing in this world that I want more than you

- *crystal*

i don't know if I could ever tell you how much I let myself fall for you

-   *below the surface*

nothing could ever replace you

-   *irreplaceable*

every time I look at you I start to hope you will be mine someday

- *beyond the future*

my name out of your mouth is like poetry

- *sweet melody*

you are more than enough.

-   *yes you*

waiting for you to walk through those doors..

- *anxiety*

I long for the time we worship the Lord together.

- *i want this with you!!*

have I ever told you how much I love you
because man oh man I DO!!

-   *100%*

You say that I'm beautiful inside and out

-   *one of the good ones*

Your personality has me desire what it would be like to do life with you

- *across the room*

I messed up so many times.
was i really worth coming back for?

-   In love

you pulled me close
and told me you loved me

-   *the chills*

they should know that if they pull us apart
we'll find our way back to each other

   -   *hope to stay together*

I want your parents to know I could love someone
even if it's the hardest thing to do
 i'll forever love you

-   *deep down*

and there you were
strong
diligent
kind
warm
handsome
and the first perfection my eyes wandered to

- *something I wish you could see*

your eyes gleamed in the sun
radiant brown rays
hoping to see all the wonders of life
I felt so lucky because you choose to lay your eyes
on me

- *gorgeous eyes*

you the guy I've always wanted in my life

    -    *do I deserve you*

I like having talks with you about how we're doing
It makes me feel reassured
about us
and me

-   *gratefulness*

our lips close to falling on each other's

- *All my*

there are a lot of things I want
but most of all I want is to be what your craving

-   I

Caressed was the word I thought of when I looked at you
It described the way your hands fall on my skin
…with your on going love

-   *continuously*

your admire the way I speak
the way my lips move to the sound of the wind
your admire the way I look
your eyes lay on mine like it was meant to be

-    *the feeling*

people said when they saw me and you together
they knew it wasn't just a regular teenage love
they said that we were different

- *what's said about us*

the first time you said "I love you"
I wondered how you were feeling
were you scared
were you excited

- *how did you feel*

it's always your eyes that make me crazy about you

- *arrogant*

just know that I would die for you
your life line is what I'll be
my loyalty is guarantee

-   *just for you love*

i don't think too much about if we're going to be okay
i know that we are a strong team that could get through anything that comes our way

- *our essence*

You said "thank you for being here for me, I really appreciate it"
I'm glad I'm here, always.

-    *text messages*

you could leave me,
break my heart and I'll still want the best for you
cause that's the kind of love you deserve even
though you made mistakes

- *Runaway*

you saw me for me when nobody else did
and that's why I fell in love with you

- *the only person I fell for*

through sickness and health
through richer or poorer
I do.
I'll be there

    -   *all the above*

I told my mom I want to marry you
with tears coming from my eyes

- *Imagine*

I've memorized my favorite song you play for me on piano
I can't get it out of my head

-   *keys*

you are a work of art i don't mind looking at

-   *art*

she will be with you till the end
she would comfort you when you try to pretend that
you're okay
she will be there when you fall down
she will be there to get you back on your feet

- *your solar system*

I'll take care of you when we're old and wrinkly
for you I shall

- *old house*

you have all my attention

- *my gold*

there are many times that I let the outside world get
to me
I regret letting it
but through those times I found you

- *the path led me to you*

you say when I'm lost
you'll be the one to rescue me

   -   *he's my compass*

think of me when you're alone
don't be afraid to call out to me
I promised you I'll be here in the times you need
someone

-   *so many promises*

if this life is all we have
would you want me to be with you till the end

-   *Our chances*

You are magnificent

- *spark*

you understand the deepest parts of me

-   *ocean*

you've had nightmares
woke up with tears dropping down your cheeks
but once you saw me you felt at peace

-   *your day dream*

you found me in the darkest and helped me bloom

   -   *changing*

the sun fell
city lights turned on
and it was just me and you

- *sugar sweet*

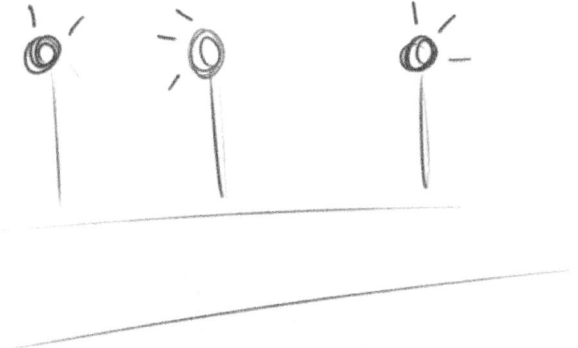

your cheek against mine while your hands are around
me
last hug of the year

-   *constellations*

Dear reader,

If you made it this far, thank you, thank you for reading a love story that I long to have. All of these poems are about a person who has impacted my life, he was always there when I was going through failure, when I lost a loved one, and when I was having trouble loving myself. I adored him for everything he did for me. I hope you find someone who will love you deeply and all of your flaws. Love takes time, don't rush what you want in love. Take time to help yourself grow, learn to love yourself before you start to love someone else. I tell you this because once you do, that person that you are longing to have, you will be able to love that person so much more than you would have.

Where to find me
Instagram @official_greyna